Hearts Aflame, Still Burning

ROSA NADINE XOCHIMILCO SÁNCHEZ

DEDICATION

For Phil:

My heart is yours, always.

ACKNOWLEDGMENTS

A huge amount of gratitude goes to my family of artists, writers, and educators, especially my mother Ann, my father Joseph, and my godparents, David and Francine. Your collective creativity has made me who I am.

Thank you to the women in my family, who have always told me to write; guiding my heart and my pen with stories of life and love and truth; to the Grandmothers: Nadine Wilhelmina, Sarita Clorinda, Norma Jaichima, and Daphne Louise; to the Nadines: Ann, Alysha, Carrie, and Eva; and to the Aunts: Geralynn Fay, Elizabeth Agnes, Rebecca Lynn, Jeanne Marie, Kathryn Louise, Mary Margaret, Theresa Karen Celeste, Maria Cecilia, Ida Linda, Lucia Beatrice, Maria, and Petra Monica.

For all the ladies in my life that give me their friendship, thank you.

To the marvelous Charles J. Orlando, Angela Owens, and William Rowel: thank you for the guidance, notes, support, and encouragement that made this publication possible.

To Nicholas Ryan Howard and Mark Meloccaro, thank you for everything. You are the best friends a girl could ever ask for. Here's to our ongoing adventures. Love you both so much.

Lastly, for anyone that truly believes in love, and drinks Romanticism straight from the bottle, let these words go from my lips to your heart.

ROSA NADINE XOCHIMILCO SÁNCHEZ

1.

I'm lost in dreams of you.
You've walked through my head
All day long.

Liquid languid lavender lights
Leaving me breathless.

A world of smiles and softness.

Of gentle words and heavy caresses.

Of kindness and desire.

Of being completely consumed by thoughts of you.

What to do, what to do
But be free
To be lost
In love.

2.

Right now I want it all.

I want your moments, your kisses on my neck.
I want your hands on my skin.

I want your voice in my ears.
I want your song in my heart.

I want your body in my bed.
I want to lose myself in your eyes.

I just want you.

3.

And in the dream
There is
No whispering
No waiting
Just fullness.

Just softness.

Just kindness.

And there you are
Dreaming
With me
Hands on my shoulders
No whispers
No waiting
No hesitation.

And all I can feel is
Your lips on my neck
In the warm silky softness of summer.

4.

I am walking with soft
Gentle steps
Safe in the twirling
Whirlwind
Patiently waiting

Dreaming of tender
Moments
And purple lights
Glowing softly gleaming

Warmer and warmer
Enflamed from the inside
Out
Burning hot and slow
Heat consuming each step

But I walk safe in the
Whirlwind
Gentle steps
The wind peeling the flame
From my skin
Making it ripe for your
Kisses

5.

Consumed and taken,
Is it so if I give myself
Freely?

I wade through uncertainty,
Grab your hand and
Find strength.

Lost in the wilderness,
The elements fade in your arms.

I am the flame that you light,
I am the fire that you quench.

Skin to skin, you are the air
I want to breathe.

6.

I want your hands on my skin
Smooth, caressing.

I want your lips on my neck
Soft, fierce.

Corseted and dainty, holding
Fast to tradition
And propriety.

I dream of you and faint.
I pull the corset tighter
Wishing it was your arms
Around me.

7.

Another lovely day in my heart.

And I have nothing but sweet
Thoughts of you.

Full of softness and sweetness
And kind-hearted love.

Giving me gentle kisses
On my neck and
Dreams of an amazing
Tomorrow.

Patience is my mantra.

8.

I dream of kind soft
Moments, of gentle words,
And light in your eyes.

I dream of butterfly kisses
Of a smoldering burn, and
My perpetual surprise.

I dream of love and
Promise, and often of all
Things true.

I dream of all
These things, but I always
Dream of you.

9.

The look in your eyes
When you are inside me

The feel of your teeth on
My skin

The pull of your hands in
My hair

The soft sweetness of your
Lips against mine

The way that you can
Completely undo me with a
Word, a touch, a whisper

And that, my love, only
Begins what I am thinking of
When it comes to you

10.

So many reasons I am happy.
So many things that bring me joy.
So many moments of absolute bliss.
So many hopes and dreams for a future together.
So many things worth waiting for.

So many purposes to practice patience.
So many feelings that consume me.
So many flames that burn within.
So many things I love about you.
So many smiles for a simple "yes."

So much more to learn and experience.
So many adventures to share.
So many reasons I'm happy.
So much love I have for you in my heart.
So so much to say…

11.

Just like a wildfire.
Burning hot and a little out of control.
With warmth leading to flame leading to burning and yearning.
Fed by sparks.
Fanned by kisses.
Taking new territory each day.
Miles and miles aflame.

With heat that only spreads.
Melts everything it touches.
Gives new meaning to the word burn.
Hotter and hotter and all consuming.
Just like a wildfire.

12.

Soft and quiet
Consuming
Delicate dreams.

I just want you
To talk to hear to touch to feel
I just want you.

Soft and quiet
Elusive
Our future life.

And I just want you
Every moment of every day
I just want you.

Soft and quiet
Forever
Our love.

13.

Like waiting for that first
Summer rain;
I look to long for your warmth.

Like bathing in silk and satin,
Curled in sweet sensation;
Drenched in want.

I sit in the downpour and watch for
Your eyes, burning hot like a flame
Consuming me with each lick of light.

Like waiting for that first
Summer rain;
I look to long for you
Lingering in love.

14.

You reach inside me
And touch me in ways one ever has.

And at the moment, I am
Lost without you…still
Quivering under twinkling lights.

I can't
Explain how happy I was to see you
Come through my door.

I try to stay
Calm, but I just
Want to run to you
Want to touch you
Want to taste you
Want to drink you in.

Right now, I am
Still lost…reveling
In the way you have made me feel,
Your taste upon my lips,
The oh so recent
Memory of your hands on my body.

Each day there is something
New for me to love about
You.

Some moment that
Makes me cherish you, that
Makes me crave you, that
Makes me want to be with you more than
Ever.

Here I lay with what
I feel are
A million of those moments
Fresh in my thoughts.

And I miss you.

I love every moment we are together
And I love being with you every moment.

15.

What have you done to me?

I have woken up in a world of want.
I want to be in your arms.
I want to make you breakfast.
I want to taste you.
I want to feel your hands in my hair.
I want to feel your tongue on my neck.
I want to lose myself in you…again and again.

But mostly I just want you next to me…

Because I want to breathe in the scent of your skin.
Because I want to see you smile.
Because I want to lose myself in your eyes.
Because I want to hear your voice caress my name.
Because I want to hold you close.
Because I want you to hold me close.
Because I belong to you…

And I am completely yours.

16.

I am so lost
In so many thoughts.
Of dreams and realities
Of patience and impatience
Of all the amazing things you make me feel.

So many times
When we are together
My words fail
Me.
All the things
I should
Say but don't
Want to
Say but can't say;
But when I do
Need to speak
I do.

And the rest
Of the time
I just try;
To tell you with my eyes
To tell you with my lips
To tell you with my body.

I love each moment
We spend together
I get lost
In your eyes.

I smile
Even now
At the way
You make
Me laugh,

My love.
I am so happy to be yours.

17.

Soft tender steps
Each toward something
Magical

Dreaming constantly of
Delicious moments
Shared

Closed eyes reveal the
Hopeful future
Intertwined

Currently losing myself
In the moment that is
Now

18.

Silver white wings
Carry my dreams
To delightfully
Fluffy
Clouds where all
I can see is
An amazing future
With you...

19.

There are times
When I crave your skin
When I want you
Desperately
When I need your touch,

There are times
When I smile gently
Thinking of you
When a kiss of the cheek
Turns me pink
When soft is everything,

There are times
When I lose myself in you
When gossamer dreams
Consume me
When dreams dance on
The edge of my reality,

There are times
When I couldn't be
Happier
When I am thrilled to be
Yours
When your love is dreams
Made real

All the time.

20.

Oh my, love
You always warm my heart.

While I began my morning with a
Flame of desire for you, I
End my night feeling the
Softly glowing embers
Of your love, equally
Full of intensity and fire.

When I read your messages
I hear your voice,
And it is like you are with me,
Whispering gently to me,
Holding me close.

From dawn to darkness my thoughts
Have been of you.
Even now, attempting sleep,
I am so full of words…

An endless stream of
Emotions and thoughts,
Made tangible
Through deliberate vocabulary, and
Free flowing stream
Of consciousness
Liquid love as I
Lie awake,

Dreaming of you.

21.

Surrounded by a kind of magic
There is tangible sparkle to the air,
And yet there is something in my heart calling out
My desire for you to be here.

With bright fireworks and colored lights
The scent of sugar coated everything in the air,
My hand looking for yours to hold, full of
My desire for you to be here.

Softly flowing dreaming longing
My face full of smiles each time I think of you near,
Full of love as well as whispers of
My desire for you to be here.

22.

Right now
I would just love
To curl myself
Around you,

Breathe in the
Soft velvet
Of your skin,

Taste your
Sweet tongue,

And become
Completely
Lost in
Your arms.

23.

So many sweet moments
Such azucar coated
Memories

Such candy dreams of
Daylight lives
So many things to hope
For

So many adventures on
The horizon
Such true love brought
New

Such amazing words
Brought soft
So many possibilities of
Bright light

So many dreamy drops of
Liquid lusciousness
Such velvet promises of
Each new day

24.

Construction takes time,
Each stone inlaid with hopes and dreams;
Specially crafted with love and heartfire,
Hearts open and emotion unbound.

Each brick on this path,
Carved delicately with desire enflamed;
Laid gently with both sets of hands,
Carefully smoothed with patient peace and hopeful promises.

Eventually the road leads home.

25.

Silken skin smoothed so softly
Hands holding hot hot heat
With wild whispers waiting wishfully
Feeling free fantasies fully fulfilled
Every entranced everything entwined enfleshed
Revealing real rapture radiant resplendent

26.

There are moments;
When all I can think about is the way you smile at me;
With kindness and love and white hot fire;
With fierce passion and gentle caresses;
Full of knowledge of moments stolen and secrets kept;
Full of flesh filled desires and wondrous wishes for the future;

There are moments;
When all I can think about is the sound of your voice;
Laden with whispered promises and tender kisses;
Thick with conflicted surprise and absolute certainty;
Wholly honey coated and sweet tasting to my soul;
Rich with dreams of melodies of a world I love;

There are moments;
When all I can imagine is the feel of your hands on my skin;
Fingertips inducing wild passions and lost breath;
Hands endlessly untangling my incessant mane;
Arms embracing me with all the love in the world;
Face always even with mine, meeting me there for every shiver and
shake;

There are moments;
When all I can think about is you;
Amazing, wonderful, and absolutely dreamy;
Inducing nothing but happiness and immense joy;
Bring my heart forth and making it shine;
And letting me dream of a future with you always in love.

27.

Sometimes I get lost in dreams;
Looking, looking, looking for you.

Dreaming of things real and surreal,
Of moments past and moments future;
Always, always, always with you.

Sometimes I get lost in dreams;
Dancing, singing, laughing with you.

Whispering of longing and loving,
Of all the things I want to have and be and share;
Always, always, always with you.

Sometimes I get lost in dreams;
Wishing, wishing, wishing for you.

Looking for fantasy magic made real,
Your hand in mine,
And all the promise of a bright new day;
Always, always, always with you.

28.

The summer sun sets,
And all I want is you
In my arms
In my bed
In my mind
In my heart.

29.

My love my love…

I long for the day
You are mine every night.

When we can have
Amazing days like today,
Everyday.

When we can share
Ridiculous meals and
Delightful desserts with
Every whim.

When I can bring you
Coffee for your late nights.

When I can curl myself
Around you, and fall asleep
To your heartbeat.

When I can awaken in your
Arms each morning.

When I can just lean over
And tell you how much you
Mean to mean instead of
Sending my words over
Waves.

I miss you my love…and

You have my
Heart…always.

30.

Full of fierce desire and
Dreams of stolen hours,
Sensory memories of your
Skin against mine; I wait
Patiently for your touch.

Moving slowly and
Endlessly circling, eyes
Locked in passionate
Longing; showing how
Much I want you.

Whispering and waiting,
Feather light kisses
Caressing my soul; my life
Moves to the beat of your
Heart.

Endless hopes and such
Happy dreams, of always
Being in your embrace; I
Belong to you.

31.

A million thoughts running
Through my head like
Some sort of verbal
Marathon;

I am in and out and in and
Out of sleep, curled in your
Warmth and your scent;

Your sounds still fresh in
My head, your sweet voice
Sings me to sleep over and
Over;

Everything we do;
Everything we are;
Everything about me still in
Complete sapphire
Sensory overload;

The word on my lips is
Love.

32.

I can almost
Taste you

Sweet
Soft

Like the nectar of sugar
Coated fruits

Like the warmth of a
Breath on a cold night

Like the soft certainty of
Promises whispered

Like fingertips feather light
Against my skin

Like dreams

Like magic

Like everything I could
Ever want

33.

I awaken
Wet eyes
Soft
Still dreaming
Wishing you were here.

I awaken
Warm skin
Soft
Still sort of sleeping
Wishing for your sweet lips.

I awaken
Gentle
Soft hands
Still wishing
Wishing you were mine
Each morning.

I awaken
Hopeful heart
Soft
Still dreaming
Wishing for everything.

34.

My face is dry
No tears.

But my heart does long
For your soft warmth.

My body craves
Your velvet embrace.

My chest is tight
With anticipation and
Impatience.

I miss you so
Much already.

My whole world
Is brighter when I can see
Your smiling eyes.

35.

Late into the night
I drift into sleep
My heart far away
Clutched in your arms

Soft smooth
Dreaming I can hear
Your sweet voice
Singing me to sleep

Night looms large
Tomorrow being welcome
As your face
Becomes reality again

And my love dances
Soaring through moonlight
To find you and wish you
Sweet sweet dreams

36.

There you fly
Into the night
And I am longing
Hands reaching out to
You.

So much love curled in
Satin sheets
With shining lights
And the scent of your skin.

Nothing so contagious as
Your laugh, as your smile,
Drawing out dimples and
Giggles, making the world
Glow.

Your love in waves and
Kisses and caresses
Flooding into my whole
Being, drawing me ever
Closer to you.

And with fluttery wings
Bathing my heart in
Shudders and shivers, I
Reach out to take your
Hand, truly yours.

37.

Morning light streams
Through,
Softly calling for the day
And I lay tangled
A mess of sheets and hair.
Laying luxurious
Balking at daybreak,
Just wanting you
To slip in close behind me
And take me in your arms.

38.

Love
Looking to the future
There is only
Love

And no amount of impatience
Brings me closer but
There is only
Love

And longing and longing
Lonely nights don't distract because
There is only
Love

And soft music wafts gently
Singing songs about how
There is only
Love

And no words can ever express
How I truly feel because
There is only
Love

39.

In the cold quiet of the morning
You whisper possibilities,

And there in those moments;
Your hand on my bare skin

I am everything I need to be.

40.

Breathing in the night,
Basking in the Bliss,
Bathed in the memory,
Of your ghostly touch.

Invisible hands caressing my skin.
Invisible lips tasting my curves.
Invisible tongue lapping at my neck.

Pushed from comfort,
Led from fear,
Fueled by desire,
Fed by love.

Invisible hands touch every inch of me.
Invisible lips sing me love songs.
Invisible tongue telling me to love you.

Breathing in the night,
Basking in the Bliss,
Longing for your warmth,
Your apparition could only stay so long.

ABOUT THE AUTHOR

Rosa Nadine Xochimilco Sánchez was born from a blend of prairie wind, smudge sticks, and blue corn enchiladas; and her sensibilities leave her bridging culture, language, space, and spirit, always guided by all of her relations. She has been writing poetry since she was four years old, and has been publishing and performing her work throughout her life.

With a reverence for pop culture, she loves Disneyland, comic books, collecting...everything, and epic culinary adventures. She lives with her mutt, Tubby, and together they live La Vie Bohème and quest for the best tacos in the City of Angels and the best tea in the Square Mile.

With the heart of a true romantic, Rosa Nadine Xochimilco Sánchez is always in love with love – and believes it is out there for everyone.